THE SUSHI BOOK

by Setsuko Yoshizuka and Shizuko Mishima

RUNNING PRESS
PHILADELPHIA · LONDON

© 2002 by Running Press

All rights reserved under the Pan-American and
International Copyright Conventions
Printed in China

9 8 7 6 5 4 3
Digit on the right indicates the number of this printing

ISBN-13: 978-0-7624-1353-9
ISBN-10: 0-7624-1353-0

Package photograpy: Foodfolio/Alamy Images
Cover design by Frances J. Soo Ping Chow
Interior illustrations by Bill Jones
Interior design by Maria Taffera Lewis
Edited by Melissa Wagner
Typography: Frutiger and Schneidler

This kit may be ordered by mail from the publisher.
Please include $2.50 for postage and handling.
But try your bookstore first!

Running Press Book Publishers
2300 Chestnut Street
Philadelphia, Pennsylvania 19103-4371

Visit us on the web!
www.runningpress.com

TABLE
OF CONTENTS

INTRODUCTION   5

SUSHI BASICS   9

    Sushi Bar Etiquette Tips   10

    How to Eat Sushi   11

    What You Need to Make Sushi   12

    Choosing Fish for Sushi   14

SUSHI RECIPES   21

    Sushi Rice   22

    Nigiri-Zushi   25

    Gunkan   28

    Maki-Zushi   30

    Temaki-Zushi   46

    Onigiri   48

    Chirashi-Zushi   50

    Pantry and Preparation Recipes 52

    Serving Suggestions   56

GLOSSARY   59

INTRO-
DUCTION

5

Sushi is perhaps the most famous Japanese food

in the world. But what exactly is meant by the word "sushi"?

Some people think that sushi refers to raw fish, but this is not

the case. Raw fish is called *sashimi* in Japan and though it can be

a component of sushi, the terms are not synonymous. In modern

Japanese cuisine, sushi indicates dishes that use sushi rice, or are

seasoned with a sweet vinegar mixture.

There are many varieties of Japanese sushi, and some don't

include raw fish. Cooked fish, shellfish, vegetables, and

various other ingredients can be combined in the many types

of sushi. However, raw fish remains one of the most essential ingredients, second only to the rice. Since Japan is surrounded by ocean, seafood has always been widely consumed in Japan. It seems only natural that this combination of raw fish and rice is a popular food in Japan.

Sushi is a healthy food. It is low in fat and high in nutrients. A typical setting of seven to nine pieces of *nigiri-zushi* contains only about 400 to 550 calories. The fish in sushi provides protein and can be a good source of omega-3 fatty acids. Needless to say, the vegetables are a great source of vitamins, and the rice provides complex carbohydrates. The dried seaweed used in *maki-zushi* is rich in iodine.

Sushi chefs in Japan go through extensive training to learn to make sushi, but it's not impossible to make sushi at home. You can use your favorite ingredients to make your own. This book and kit will provide you with some basic tools and instructions for making your own sushi creations. Have fun!

SUSHI BASICS

Sushi did not originate in Japan. It is said that sushi originated in Southeast Asia, and that the Chinese brought it to Japan in the seventh century. In the beginning, people preserved raw fish in salt and kept it for months. This fermented fish is the origin of sushi. Unlike modern sushi, vinegar wasn't used. The sourness came from the fermentation.

In the sixteenth century, people began to use rice and salt to speed up the fermentation of fish. This type of sushi, called *nare-zushi*, is still cooked in Japan today. It takes weeks to make *nare-zushi*. In the seventeenth century, improvements occurred when people began to add vinegar to season the rice instead of fermenting the raw fish, enabling sushi to be made much more quickly. Vinegar had the added bonus of acting as an effective antiseptic with a sterilizing function. Therefore, it's logical to add vinegar to sushi, which is usually made with uncooked fish.

Rolled sushi, called *maki-zushi*, appeared in the eighteenth century, and people started to experiment with many ingredients and fillings. The oval-shaped sushi topped with a slice of raw fish, called *nigiri-zushi*, appeared in the nineteenth century. Since it's easy to eat *nigiri-zushi*, it became popular quickly, and now *nigiri-zushi* is the most popular type of sushi in the world. It is the king of sushi.

SUSHI BAR ETIQUETTE TIPS

Here are some etiquette tips to employ when you'd prefer to let someone else do the sushi preparation.

- Clean your hands with an *oshibori* (hot towel), then order a drink. Green tea (called *agari* in sushi restaurants) is the best drink with sushi.

- You can order a sushi combination with a fixed price, or order your favorite sushi pieces à la carte.
- It's polite to ask the sushi chef for his or her recommendation of the day.
- If you are not ordering a combination of sushi from the menu, it is better to order a few kinds of sushi at a time instead of ordering a lot at once.
- Try not to ask the sushi chef to bring you things, like a drink or your bill. Talk to the waitress or host about these matters.
- It's considered polite to offer to buy your sushi chef a drink if he or she is doing a good job.

HOW TO EAT SUSHI

1. Clean your hands with an *oshibori* (hot towel).

2. Put soy sauce for dipping in the small dish.

3. If you like, mix a bit of *wasabi* (japanese horseradish) with the soy sauce.

4. When you eat *nigiri-zushi,* pick up one sushi piece between

TIPS

- Don't put too much soy sauce in the small dish. It's better to add as you need it.

- Don't dip a whole piece of sushi into the soy sauce. The rice tends to fall apart.

- Eat pieces of pickled ginger between different kinds of sushi. It helps to clean your mouth and enhance the flavors. Use chopsticks to eat ginger.

your thumb and middle finger, putting the index finger on top. (It's common to use your fingers to eat sushi.) Dip the end of the *neta* (ingredients/ fish slice side) into the soy sauce rather than the rice. Bring the sushi to your mouth and bite in half. Before your next bite, again dip the *neta* side in the soy sauce.

5. When you eat *maki-zushi* (rolled sushi), place the whole piece in your mouth if you can. *Maki-zushi* falls apart easily when it is bitten.

WHAT YOU NEED TO MAKE SUSHI

Our kit includes essential items you need to make sushi, including:

- a *makisu*, a rolling mat for making m*aki-zushi*;
- a paddle for handling sushi rice; and

- a plastic mold to help form rice for *nigiri-zushi* and *onigiri* (rice balls).

The kit also includes elements which are essential for serving and presenting the sushi after you've made it, including:
- chopsticks;
- dipping bowls for serving soy sauce; and
- a serving plate.

In addition to these non-food items, you'll need several food-ingredients to prepare sushi at home. These ingredients include:
- Japanese rice (medium grained);
- sushi vinegar (you can purchase seasoned sushi vinegar at a store, but it's just as simple to make it at home using rice vinegar—see How to Make Sushi Rice, step 1, on page 23);
- *nori* (sheets of dried seaweed);
- soy sauce, which may be used as a dipping sauce for many varieties of sushi;
- *wasabi* (Japanese horseradish), which is put in *nigiri-zushi* or mixed with soy sauce for dipping sushi;
- *gari* (pickled ginger), which is eaten between bites of sushi to

refresh the mouth for each new taste (see more on *gari* on page 52); and

• green tea, which is the best accompaniment when eating sushi. Make the tea strong and hot.

CHOOSING FISH FOR SUSHI

There are numerous types of fish that can be used in sushi, many of which are listed in this chapter. Take time to familiarize yourself with the various types of fish used in sushi, and talk to your fishmonger about the seasonality of specific fish. It's always a good idea to ask him or her to recommend the freshest and best fish—if you explain that you are using it for sushi, he or she will most likely point you in the right direction.

When choosing fish and seafood for making sushi, freshness is of the utmost importance. Here are some tips on spotting the freshest catches:

FISH

• To help ensure freshness, buy whole fish and fillet them at home when possible. When selecting larger fish, it may be too expensive to buy the whole thing, so choose fillets and smaller cuts that are moist, with good color.

- Make sure the fish has bright, clear eyes. There shouldn't be any blood or cloudiness present in the eyes, and they shouldn't be sunken into the head of the fish.
- Make sure that the scales are glossy, and that the gills are a bright-red color.
- Poke your fish gently, making sure that the flesh springs back. The flesh of the fish should feel firm and elastic.
- A fresh fish smells fresh—avoid fish with a strong "fishy" odor.
- When choosing tuna fillets, make sure that the flesh has distinct stripes in it around the belly, and clear red without strips in other parts.
- White-colored flesh should be almost transparent.
- The back is the most succulent part of most fish. Tuna represents an exception—the tender, fatty belly area is most sought-after.
- If you are using frozen fish, allow it to thaw as slowly as possible, perhaps overnight in the refrigerator. Don't try to speed the process by soaking it in water, which will strip away flavor from your fish.

SEAFOOD

- **Shellfish:** It's always best to buy live shellfish. Pry open the shell—it should close by itself. If the shell remains open, the mollusk is dead.
- **Shrimp:** It is best to use live shrimp when making sushi, so pick out shrimp that are active and have good color. Shrimp can still be used even if it is no longer alive, so long as their stripes remain distinct—they should not be blurred together.
- **Squid:** To make sure that squid is still alive when it is purchased, check that the skin around the eyes is clear blue, and that the suckers respond when touched.
- **Octopus:** Octopus is usually already boiled before it is sold. Talk to your fishmonger to see whether it can be used for sushi.

RAW FISH

Common raw fish used for sushi are *maguro* (tuna), *toro* (fatty belly part of tuna), *saba* (mackerel), *ika* (squid), *hamachi* (yellowtail), and *hotate* (scallop).

See the following list for instructions on buying and cutting these fish for sushi.

MAGURO (TUNA) AND *TORO* (BELLY OF TUNA)

1. Buy a block of fresh tuna and shape it into a rectangle.

2. Slice the tuna into smaller rectangular pieces (1½ by 2 inches) for *nigiri-zushi*.

3. Always cut tuna diagonally, against gristles.

IKA (SQUID)

1. Buy fresh, clear squid.

2. Take out the guts, the head, and legs. Peel the skin.

3. Cut the squid open into a flat piece. Cut it into thirds vertically.

4. Cut each sheet of squid into smaller rectangular pieces (1½ by 2 inches) for *nigiri-zushi*.

SABA (MACKEREL)

1. Buy extremely fresh mackerel since this fish goes bad easily. Check for a pointed shape to the stomach, and an upright tail—a sagging tail is a clue that the fish is not fresh.

2. Take the guts out and fillet the fish.

3. Soak the slices in rice vinegar for one hour.

4. Wipe the fish well with a paper towel and peel the skin. Slice the fish into smaller pieces diagonally.

HOTATE (SCALLOPS)

1. Buy fresh scallops and wash them in saltwater.

2. Remove the white part on the side.

3. Cut each scallop in half horizontally and pour boiling water over the slices. Dry the slices with a paper towel.

COOKED FISH

Common cooked fish used in sushi are *tako* (octopus), *ebi* (shrimp), *anago* (conger eel), *kani* (crab), and *kanikama* (imitation crab).

TAKO (OCTOPUS)

1. Buy boiled octopus and wash well.

2. Diagonally cut the octopus into smaller rectangular pieces (1½ by 2 inches).

EBI (SHRIMP)

1. Buy medium-sized shrimp. Wash the shrimp and remove the heads.

2. Insert a bamboo skewer through each shrimp, from the head to the tail.

3. Boil the shrimp in salted water for about 3 minutes. Remove from the heat and drain the shrimp.

4. Cool the shrimp, then remove the skewer and the shell.

5. To flatten the shrimp, cut each horizontally along the belly and press it open. Remove the vein, wash, and dry with a paper towel.

ANAGO (CONGER EEL)

1. Buy prepared eel and boil it in salted water for a couple minutes.

2. Mix 3 tablespoons of sugar, ⅓ cup of soy sauce, 3 tablespoons of *saké* (rice wine), and 2 cups of hot water in a frying pan. Add the eel, and simmer for 10 minutes.

3. Cut the cooked eel in half horizontally and further cut the pieces vertically into smaller rectangular pieces (1½ by 2 inches).

SUSHI RECIPES

Now you are ready to begin your adventures in sushi-making. While you may be very familiar with eating sushi, it's is a true art form to actually create it. It's important to master the basics, such as preparing proper sushi rice, and to have your *wasabi* and ginger waiting in the wings for serving. With step-by-step instructions, you are just pages away from making your favorite *nigiri*, *gunkan*, *maki*, *temaki*, and *onigiri*. Once you've mastered the recipes in this book, feel free to experiment, as there are no wrong combinations. If you and your guests enjoy your sushi, that's all that matters. Happy rolling!

SUSHI RICE

Learning to make the rice properly is the first step

in creating great-tasting sushi. Japanese rice is a medium-

grained rice that gets sticky when it is cooked.

Long-grained American rice can't be used for sushi

because it is drier and doesn't stick together.

HOW TO MAKE SUSHI RICE

Ingredients

⅓ cup unseasoned rice vinegar*

2 tablespoons sugar

1 teaspoon salt

3 cups Japanese rice

3¼ cups water

Special Equipment

Saucepan or rice cooker

Paddle or spatula

* If using seasoned sushi vinegar, omit salt and sugar from the ingredients.

Sushi-oke (shallow wooden bowl), large plate, or glass
or plastic mixing bowl

Handheld fan

MAKES ABOUT 4 CUPS

1. If using unseasoned rice vinegar, prepare sushi vinegar by mixing rice vinegar, sugar, and salt in a small saucepan. Cook over low heat and until the sugar dissolves. Cool the vinegar mixture.

2. Put the rice in a bowl and wash it with cold water. Repeat washing until the water becomes clear. Drain the rice in a colander and set aside.

3. Place the rice in a medium saucepan or rice cooker and add water. Let the rice soak in the water for 30 minutes to 1 hour. One hour is ideal.

4. If you are cooking the rice on the stove, cover with a lid and bring to a boil over high heat. Turn the heat down very low and cook 15 to 20 minutes or

---

TIPS

- Add vinegar mixture to the rice when the rice is still hot.

- Cool the rice quickly using a fan so that it will look shiny.

- Use a paddle or spatula to mix the rice, using a cut-and-fold motion so that you don't smash the rice grains.

---

until the water is almost gone. Remove the pan from the heat and let it steam for 10 to 15 minutes. If you are using an electric rice cooker, don't worry about adjusting the heat, but let the cooked rice steam before you open the lid.

5. Use a paddle to spread the hot rice into a large plate or a special wooden bowl called a *sushi-oke*. Avoid using metallic bowls unless they are covered with enamel or made of stainless steel, as they will react with the acid in the vinegar to create undesirable flavor.

6. Sprinkle the vinegar mixture over the rice, and use a paddle to fold it into the rice. Be careful not to break or smash the individual grains. As you work with the mixture, use a fan to help to cool the rice and remove the moisture. This will give it a shiny look.

7. Once the vinegar has been mixed in, the sushi rice is ready! It's best to use it right away.

NIGIRI-ZUSHI

This oval-shaped sushi is probably the type

that most people first think of when sushi is mentioned—

a hand-pressed mound of rice topped

with a dab of *wasabi* and a slice of raw fish, shellfish,

or other ingredients. Popular types of *nigiri-zushi* are

maguro (tuna), *toro* (belly of tuna), *hamachi* (yellowtail),

ebi (shrimp), *tamago* (omelet), *anago* (conger eel), *ika*

(squid), *tako* (octopus), and *hotategai* (scallop).

In Japan, *nigiri-zushi* is commonly served at sushi bars.

BASIC STEPS FOR MAKING NIGIRI-ZUSHI

Ingredients

Sushi Rice (see recipe on page 22)

Toppings of your choice

Wasabi (Japanese horseradish)

Special Equipment

Small bowl of seasoned rice vinegar

Sushi mold (optional)

1. Wet your palms and fingers with the seasoned rice vinegar used to make sushi rice.

2. Take about two tablespoons of sushi rice in your hand and shape it into an oval mound. Beginners may wish to use a mold like the one provided in this kit to help form the rice into the correctly-sized oval.

TIP

• Be judicious when adding *wasabi* to your *nigiri-zushi*. Guests can sometimes forget that the piece already has *wasabi* and add more, much to their discomfort.

---

3. Take a slice of whatever topping you prefer (tuna, yellowtail, eel, etc.) in the other hand and put a dab of *wasabi* on top.

4. Place the oval-shaped sushi rice on top of the topping. (The *wasabi* should be sandwiched between the rice and the topping.) Gently press the topping to the rice, using your fingers.

5. Turn the sushi over so that the rice is on the bottom. Reshape the sushi by pressing with your index finger and gently squeezing it in the palm of your hand until it has the shape you prefer.

GUNKAN

Gunkan is a kind of *nigiri-zushi* where the rice

is wrapped in a strip of *nori* (dried seaweed).

Toppings are placed on the rice,

and the seaweed helps them to stay in place.

Popular *gunkan* are *uni* (sea urchin)

and *ikura* (salmon roe).

BASIC STEPS
FOR MAKING GUNKAN

Ingredients

Nori (dried seaweed)

Sushi Rice (see recipe on page 22)

Toppings of your choice

Special Equipment

Small bowl of seasoned rice vinegar

Sushi mold (optional)

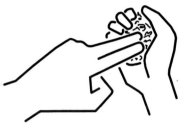

1. Cut a sheet of *nori* into thin long strips about 1-inch wide.

2. Wet your palms and fingers with the sushi vinegar mixture.

3. Take about 2 tablespoons of sushi rice in your hand and shape it into an oval mound. Beginners may wish to use a mold like the one provided in this kit to help form the rice.

29

4. Wrap the sides of the mound with a strip of *nori*. The shiny side of the *nori* should face out.

5. Secure the ends of the *nori* with some mashed grains of rice.

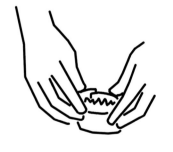

6. Place the topping in the hollow cavity on top of the rice.

MAKI-ZUSHI

Maki-zushi is rolled in a sheet of dried seaweed, or *nori*.

Maki-zushi is usually cut into rounds and served.

(*Maki* means "roll" in Japanese.) There are many kinds

of *maki-zushi*, depending on the fillings. Some popular

types include California Rolls, Spicy Tuna Rolls,

Kappa-Maki, and others. *Maki-zushi* is commonly packed

in lunch boxes in Japan. Some popular combinations follow

the step-by-step method, but you can use just about

any filling that you prefer. Be creative!

BASIC STEPS
FOR MAKING MAKI-ZUSHI

Ingredients

Full-size *nori* sheet (large rectangle)

Sushi Rice (see recipe on page 22)

Your favorite fillings (cut into strips)

Special Equipment

    Makisu (rolling mat)

    Plastic wrap (optional)

    Paddle or spatula

1. Prepare fillings.

2. Put a *nori* sheet on top of a *makisu* (rolling mat) with the shiny side on the bottom. (You may cover the *makisu* with plastic wrap to help keep it clean).

3. Spread the sushi rice on top of the *nori* sheet using the paddle. Leave a ½-inch strip uncovered at the end of the *nori*.

4. Place the ingredients lengthwise on the rice.

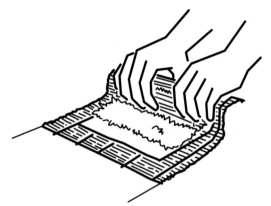

5. Roll the mat away from you, using your fingers to help hold the ingredients in place. Press forward to shape the sushi into a cylinder. Grip the rolled mat firmly with both hands, then remove the sushi.

6. Cut the rolled sushi into bite-sized pieces. Wipe the knife with a wet cloth before you slice, and make the cut with one, swift motion rather than sawing back and forth.

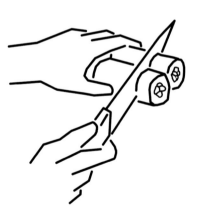

KAPPA-MAKI
(CUCUMBER ROLL)

Ingredients

1 cucumber

2 sheets of *nori* (dried seaweed), cut in half

4 cups Sushi Rice (see recipe on page 22)

MAKES 4 ROLLS (ABOUT 32 SMALL PIECES)

1. Cut the cucumber into long, thin sticks.

2. Put half a *nori* sheet on top of a *makisu* (rolling mat) with the shiny side on the bottom. (You may cover the *makisu* with plastic wrap to help keep it clean).

3. Spread the sushi rice on top of the *nori* sheet using a paddle or spatula. Leave a ½-inch strip uncovered at the end of the *nori*.

4. Place the cucumber lengthwise on the rice.

5. Roll the mat away from you, using your fingers to hold the ingredients in place. Press forward to shape the sushi into a cylinder. Grip the rolled mat firmly, then remove the sushi.

6. Cut the rolled sushi into bite-sized pieces. Wipe the knife with a wet cloth before you slice it, and make the cut with one, swift motion rather than sawing back and forth.

TEKKA-MAKI
(RAW TUNA ROLL)

Ingredients

4 ounces raw tuna

2 sheets of *nori* (dried seaweed), cut in half

4 cups Sushi Rice (see recipe on page 22)

MAKES 4 ROLLS (ABOUT 32 SMALL PIECES)

1. Cut the tuna into long, thin sticks. Set aside.

2. Put half a *nori* sheet on top of a *makisu* (rolling mat) with the shiny side on the bottom. (You may cover the *makisu* with plastic wrap to help keep it clean).

3. Spread the sushi rice on top of the *nori* sheet using the paddle. Leave a ½-inch strip uncovered at the end of the *nori*.

4. Place the tuna lengthwise on the rice.

5. Roll the mat away from you, using your fingers to hold ingredients in place. Press forward to shape the sushi into a cylinder. Grip the rolled mat firmly with both hands, then remove the sushi.

6. Cut the rolled sushi into bite-sized pieces. Wipe the knife with a wet cloth before you slice it, and make the cut with one, swift motion rather than sawing back and forth.

FUTO-MAKI (THICK ROLL)

Ingredients

1 ounce *kampyo* (dried gourd strips)

8 dried shiitake mushrooms

⅔ cup Dashi Stock (see recipe on page 55)

2 tablespoons sugar

1 tablespoon *mirin* (sweet rice wine)

3 tablespoons soy sauce

1 omelet (see recipe on page 53)

1 cucumber

4 sheets of *nori* (dried seaweed)

4 cups Sushi Rice (see recipe on page 22)

MAKES 4 ROLLS (ABOUT 32 SMALL PIECES)

1. Wash and soak *kampyo* and dried shiitake mushrooms in
   water for an hour before cooking.
2. Slice the shiitakes. Cut the *kampyo* into 8-inch pieces.
3. Combine Dashi Stock, sugar, *mirin*, and soy sauce in a medium
   saucepan and cook over low heat.
4. Add the shiitake slices and *kampyo* to the saucepan and simmer for about one hour, then remove from heat. Remove the

shiitake slices and *kampyo* from the liquid, and cool. When they've reached room temperature, cut into thin, 1-inch-long pieces. Set aside.

5. Cut omelet into long sticks. Set aside.

6. Cut cucumber into long sticks. Set aside.

7. Put a sheet of *nori*, shiny side down, on a rolling mat which can be covered with plastic wrap to help keep it clean. Spread the sushi rice on top of the *nori* sheet.

8. Place the shitakes, *kampyo*, omelet, and cucumber lengthwise on the rice.

9. Roll the mat away from you, using your fingers to help hold the ingredients in place. Press forward to shape the sushi into a cylinder. Grip the rolled mat firmly with both hands, then remove the sushi.

10. Cut the rolled sushi into bite-sized pieces. Wipe the knife with a wet cloth before you slice it, and make the cut with one, swift motion rather than sawing back and forth. The rolls will be very thick.

CALIFORNIA ROLL

Ingredients

1 avocado

¾ cup crab meat or imitation crab

1 tablespoon mayonnaise

Salt (to taste)

4 sheets of *nori* (dried seaweed)

4 cups Sushi Rice (see recipe on page 22)

Sesame seeds, for topping

MAKES 4 ROLLS (ABOUT 32 SMALL PIECES)

1. Peel an avocado and mash it or cut it into strips, depending upon your preference.

2. Mix the crabmeat and the mayonnaise.

3. Salt the avocado and the crabmeat mixture to taste.

4. Place a *nori* sheet shiny side down on top of a rolling mat, which can be covered with plastic wrap to help keep it clean. Spread the sushi rice on top of the *nori* sheet and sprinkle sesame seeds over the rice.

5. Place the avocado and crabmeat lengthwise on the rice.

6. Roll the mat away from you, using your fingers to hold the

TIP

• For some added crunch, consider adding cucumber or asparagus to your California rolls. Rather than sesame seeds, you can roll your sushi in roe.

ingredients in place. Press forward to shape the sushi into a cylinder. Grip the rolled mat firmly with both hands, then remove the sushi.

7. Cut the rolled sushi into bite-sized pieces. Wipe the knife with a wet cloth before you slice it, and make the cut with one, swift motion rather than sawing back and forth.

INSIDE-OUT CALIFORNIA ROLL

Ingredients

4 cups Sushi Rice (see recipe on page 22)

4 sheets of *nori* (dried seaweed)

1 avocado

¾ cup crab meat or imitation crab

1 tablespoon mayonnaise

Salt (to taste)

Sesame seeds for topping

MAKES 4 ROLLS (ABOUT 32 SMALL PIECES)

1. Peel an avocado and mash it or cut it into strips, according to your preference.
2. Mix the crabmeat and the mayonnaise.
3. Salt the avocado and the crabmeat mixture to taste.
4. Put a *nori* sheet with the shiny side down on top of a rolling mat covered with plastic wrap.
5. Spread the sushi rice on top of the *nori* sheet.
6. Sprinkle sesame seeds over the rice.
7. Turn the sushi layer over so that the *nori* is on top.
8. Place the avocado and crab meat lengthwise on the *nori*.

9. Roll the mat away from you, using your fingers to help hold the ingredients in place. Press forward to shape the sushi into a cylinder. Grip the rolled mat firmly with both hands, then remove the sushi.

10. Cut the rolled sushi into bite-sized pieces. Wipe the knife with a wet cloth before you slice it, and make the cut with one, swift motion rather than sawing back and forth.

SPICY TUNA ROLL

Ingredients

½ pound fresh raw tuna

1 tablespoon mayonnaise

½ teaspoon *togarashi* (Japanese hot pepper)

4 sheets of *nori* (dried seaweed)

4 cups Sushi Rice (see recipe on page 22)

1 tablespoon sesame seeds

MAKES 4 ROLLS (ABOUT 32 SMALL PIECES)

1. Chop tuna into small pieces and mix with mayonnaise and *togarashi*.

2. Put a *nori* sheet shiny side down on top of a *makisu* (rolling mat), which can be covered in plastic wrap to help keep it clean. Spread the sushi rice on top of the *nori* sheet.

3. Sprinkle the sesame seeds on top of the sushi rice.

4. Place the tuna mixture lengthwise on the rice.

TIP

• This is a favorite of sushi bars and restaurants everywhere. When serving sushi at a dinner or party, be sure to include this zesty roll.

5. Roll the mat away from you, using your fingers to help hold the ingredients in place. Press forward to shape the sushi into a cylinder. Grip the rolled mat firmly with both hands, then remove the sushi.

6. Cut the rolled sushi into bite-sized pieces. Wipe the knife with a wet cloth before you slice it, and make the cut with one, swift motion rather than sawing back and forth.

TERIYAKI CHICKEN ROLL

Ingredients

Teriyaki Chicken Breasts (see recipe on page 44)

4 sheets of *nori* (dried seaweed)

4 cups Sushi Rice (see recipe on page 22)

Teriyaki Sauce (see recipe on page 45)

MAKES 4 ROLLS (ABOUT 32 SMALL PIECES)

1. Allow Teriyaki Chicken Breasts to cool to room temperature.

2. Put a *nori* sheet shiny side down on top of a rolling mat, which can be covered with plastic wrap to help keep it clean. Spread the sushi rice on top of the *nori* sheet.

3. Place the chicken chunks lengthwise on the rice. Put a little bit of Teriyaki Sauce on top of the chicken.

4. Roll the mat away from you, using your fingers to hold the ingredients in place. Press forward to shape sushi into a cylinder. Grip the rolled mat firmly, then remove the sushi.

5. Cut the rolled sushi into bite-sized pieces. Wipe the knife with a wet cloth before you slice, and make the cut with one, swift motion rather than sawing back and forth.

TERIYAKI CHICKEN BREASTS

Ingredients

2 chicken breasts

2 tablespoons *saké* (rice wine)

4 tablespoons soy sauce

4 tablespoons *mirin* (sweet rice wine)

2 tablespoons sugar

Vegetable oil (for frying)

MAKES 2 SERVINGS

1. Cut chicken breasts into small chunks.

2. Combine the *saké*, soy sauce, *mirin*, and sugar in a large glass or plastic bowl with a lid. Add the chicken chunks to the mixture, cover, and marinate in the refrigerator for at least 30 minutes.

3. Heat a small amount of vegetable oil in a large frying pan. Add the marinated chicken to the pan and sauté on low heat until cooked through.

TERIYAKI SAUCE

Ingredients

½ cup soy sauce

½ cup *mirin* (sweet rice wine)

2 tablespoons sugar (adjust the amount of sugar
depending on your preference)

MAKES 1 CUP

1. Combine all ingredients in a
   small saucepan. Bring to a
   boil, then remove from heat.
2. Cool the mixture. Sauce can
   be stored in a clean glass
   bottle in the refrigerator.

TIP

• Teriyaki Sauce is extremely versa-
tile. Unused sauce can be used for
sushi or for basting or marinating
chicken, beef, salmon, or nearly any
kind of main dish. Experiment.

TEMAKI-ZUSHI

This simple sushi roll, often called a hand-roll in English,

is created by hand-wrapping several ingredients

of your choice in a sheet of seaweed.

It is cone-shaped, and quick to make. *Temaki-zushi*

can be fun to make at parties. Just prepare the sushi rice

and have a variety of cut ingredients on a large plate.

Each guest can choose his or her

favorite ingredients to make a personalized hand-roll.

BASIC STEPS FOR MAKING TEMAKI-ZUSHI

Ingredients

Sushi Rice (see recipe on page 22)

Sheets of *nori* (dried seaweed)

Your favorite fillings: *maguro* (raw tuna), cucumber,

tamago (omelet), *ika* (squid), crab, shrimp, lettuce,

ikura (salmon roe), etc.

Special Equipment

Paddle or spatula

1. Make sushi rice and put it in a large bowl or on a large plate. Meanwhile, cut the fillings of your choice into sticks (3 inches in length) and place them on another large plate.
2. Cut a sheet of *nori* into quarters.
3. Provide a paddle with the rice for use in scooping.
4. Place a small amount of sushi rice on top of a piece of *nori*. Pick one or two fillings from the plate and put them on top of the sushi rice. Roll the *nori* into a cone shape to wrap the fillings and rice. Eat!

ONIGIRI

Onigiri, hand-shaped round or triangular balls of rice,

is a very popular food in Japan. It's easy to eat

and is often taken on picnics or for lunch.

You can either use your hands or the mold included

in the kit to make *onigiri.*

HOW TO MAKE ONIGIRI

Ingredients

Salt to taste

1 salmon fillet

4 cups Sushi Rice (see recipe on page 22), still warm

1 tablespoon white sesame seeds

2 sheets *nori* (seaweed)

Special Equipment

Sushi mold (optional)

MAKES 8 RICE BALLS

1. Sprinkle salt over the salmon and let sit in the refrigerator for 30 minutes.

2. Grill or fry the salmon fillet until the edges are a little burned. After the salmon cools, flake it into small pieces and set aside.

3. In a large bowl, combine the warm, cooked rice, salmon flakes, and sesame seeds.

4. Wet your hands in water so that the rice won't stick to your hands, then put a pinch of salt on your hands and grab about a ½ cup of warm rice. Form the rice into a round or a triangle shape by pressing lightly with your both palms. You might also shape the rice with the mold in the kit.

5. Cut a sheet of *nori* into quarters, then wrap the rice with a small sheet of *nori*. The *nori* doesn't have to be cut in the shape of the rice—it will stick well and cover the rice ball just fine.

CHIRASHI-ZUSHI

Chirashi means "scattered," and that's just what this type of

sushi is—an improvisation of fish and vegetables placed on a

bed of rice, usually served in individual lacquer bowls or boxes

(but any wide, deep dish will suffice). With its contrasting,

bright colors, *chirashi* can be a very attractive dish

to serve. For this dish, the sky's the limit—try combining any

(or all!) of your favorite sushi ingredients for a beautiful,

imaginative presentation. Here is your chance to get creative!

BASIC STEPS FOR MAKING CHIRASHI-ZUSHI

Ingredients

1 omelet (see recipe on page 53)

8 medium shrimp

1 medium cucumber

2½ cups sushi rice (see recipe on page 22)

1 tablespoon sesame seeds

MAKES 4 SERVINGS

1. Cut the omelet into thin shreds.

2. Prepare shrimp, following the instructions in the Choosing Fish for Sushi section on page 14.

3. Cut cucumber into pieces about 2-inches long, then slice each piece horizontally into rectangular pieces. Cut the cucumber into thin shreds.

4. Spread sushi rice on a flat plate.

5. Spread sesame seeds over the rice.

6. Spread cucumber and egg shreds over the rice.

7. Place shrimp on top. Serve.

PANTRY AND PREPARATION RECIPES

A little preparation will make sushi a breeze.

Many of the ingredients can be made well in advance, such

as Pickled Ginger or Dashi Stock, so long as it is frozen.

Keeping rice, *wasabi* paste, and *nori* on hand

is also a good idea for the sushi enthusiast. Buy the fresh

ingredients you need at your local market and tonight's

dinner will be a delicious adventure.

PICKLED GINGER

Pickled ginger, called *gari* in Japanese, is served with sushi. Eating pieces of pickled ginger between different kinds of sushi helps to clean your mouth and enhance the flavors of the ingredients.

Ingredients

2 large ginger roots

1 teaspoon salt

1 cup rice vinegar

5 to 7 tablespoons sugar

1. Peel the ginger root. Cut it into medium-sized pieces, and combine it with the salt. Let marinate for 30 minutes.

2. Place the ginger into a jar with a lid.

3. Mix the rice vinegar and sugar in a pan and bring to a boil. Pour the hot mixture into the jar with the ginger. Cool, then cover with a lid and place in the refrigerator.

4. The ginger will be ready in about one week, or once the color changes to light pink. Slice thinly to serve. The pickled ginger lasts about a month when refrigerated.

SUSHI OMELET

Ingredients

6 eggs

2 tablespoons sugar

¼ cup Dashi Stock (see recipe on page 55)

Vegetable oil

MAKES 1 OMELET

1. In a small bowl, beat the eggs and add sugar and Dashi Stock.

2. Heat little bit of vegetable oil in a square omelet pan on medium heat.

3. Pour a thin layer of egg mixture into the pan. When the egg mixture is firm, use chopsticks to roll the egg mixture toward you, forming a block that is about 2 inches wide when you are through. Push the block to the end of the pan farthest from you.

4. Oil the empty part of the pan and pour more egg mixture in the pan. Lift the block to make sure that the mixture coats the pan underneath it.

5. Cook until firm, then use chopsticks again to fold the egg mixture toward you, making the initial egg block even thicker. Push the block to the end of the pan farthest from you. Repeat this process until the egg mixture is gone.

6. When the omelet is done, remove it from the pan and put it on a bamboo mat covered in plastic wrap. Use the mat to shape the omelet into a rectangle. When the omelet is cool, remove it from the rolling mat and cut it into small rectangular slices for use in *nigiri-zushi* or *futo-maki*.

DASHI STOCK

Ingredients

4 cups of water

6 inches *konbu* (kelp)

⅓ cup of *katsuobushi* (dried bonito flakes)

MAKES 4 CUPS

1. Put water in a stock pot and soak *konbu* for one to two hours.
2. Heat the water on low heat and remove the *konbu* just before the water boils.
3. Add the *katsuobushi* to the boiling water and immediately turn off the heat. Strain the broth.

SERVING SUGGESTIONS

Sushi is terrific as both an *hors d'oeuvre* or an entrée,

and regardless of what course you are planning

on serving it for, it's critical to make sure

that you've prepared enough sushi to serve your guests.

In general, if you are serving sushi as an *hors d'oeuvre* or appe-
tizer, plan on 4 to 5 pieces per person. Any combination is accept-
able but remember that guests will want to try a nice variety of
rolls, etc. For a main course, plan on serving a combination of 4
finger rolls and 6 pieces of rolled sushi. Obviously, it's nice to
offer a sampler of various sushi, so play with different forms of
sushi as well as different ingredients, such as vegetarian, omelet,
and seafood.

PREPARATION & SERVING

If you're throwing a sushi extravaganza, advance planning is necessary. On the day of the event, prepare the sushi rice, chill the ginger, and prepare and refrigerate the ingredients in advance.

Just before assembly, mix up *wasabi*, dilute rice vinegar with water, and assemble the ingredients and materials. Use the rolling mat, rice paddle, and mold in this kit in your sushi preparation. Scissors are also handy to have nearby so you can easily cut your *nori* as needed. You are now ready to create your sushi.

57

Fill the matching dipping trays with soy sauce for your guests. Make sure you have small piles of ginger and *wasabi* within easy reach of your guest's chopsticks. Use a serving plate to display and serve rolls and sushi pieces. Bring out new rolls as they are ready. You might even want to set the mood with a Japanese-inspired table setting and music. Serve *saké*, green tea, or Japanese beer (such as Kirin). Be as creative in your presentation as you are with your sushi. Enjoy!

GLOSSARY

Abura-age: deep-fried bean curd

Age-mono: deep-frying food

Aji-ponzu: a type of Japanese sour dipping sauce that usually includes vinegar, soy sauce, and citrus fruit juice

Aka oroshi: grated daikon radish and Japanese red pepper (*togarashi*)

Akami: dark meat from the middle of a fish

Anago: conger eel

Awabi: abalone

Awasezu: vinegar mixture

Burdock (Gobo): a Japanese root vegetable

Buri: yellowtail kingfish

Chiai: dark outer meat of a fish

Chirashi-zushi: scattered sushi—meat, fish, vegetables, and omelet arranged over sushi rice and served in bowls

Chimaki: rice dumplings wrapped in bamboo leaves

Daikon: Japanese radish, sometimes called giant white or mooli radish

Ebi: shrimp or lobster

Furikake: mixed seasoning to be served with rice

Futo-maki: large sushi roll

Gari: pickled ginger

Goma: sesame seeds

Go-mai oraoshi: five-fillet cut for fish; best fillet method for flat fish and particularly large fish

Gunkan-maki: "battleship" sushi; hand-formed sushi consisting of a pillow of rice surrounded by a wall of seaweed and topped with roe

Hako zushi: boxed or pressed sushi; preparation requires a pressing box to create blocks of sushi that resemble finger sushi

Hamachi: (young) yellowtail

Hangiri: rice tub for sushi rice

Hirame: halibut

Hocho: knives

Horenso: spinach

Hoso-maki: small sushi rolls

Hotate-gai: scallops

Ika: squid (calamari)

Ikura: salmon roe

Inari-zushi: stuffed, deep-fried bean curd pouch

Itamae: a cook or chef

Kabayaki: cooked conger eel

Kaiware: small, thin radish

Kaki: oysters

Kamaboko: fish cake

Kampyo: strips of dried gourd

Kani: crab

Kappa-maki: small sushi roll filled with cucumber

Katsuo: bonito (bonita)

Kohada/Konoshiro: gizzard shad

Kome: matured, short-grain rice

Konbu: kelp

Maguro: bluefin tuna

Maki: rolled sushi

Makisu: bamboo rolling mat

61

Mirin: sweet rice wine for cooking

Mirugai: horse clam

Miso: fermented soy bean paste

Mushi-zushi: steamed sushi

Nare-zushi: fermented sushi

Natto: fermented soybeans

Nigiri-zushi: squeezed or pressed sushi (finger sushi)

Ninjin: carrot

Nori: seaweed paper

Oba: Japanese basil

Ocha: green tea

O-hashi: chopsticks

Onigiri: rice ball

Oshi zushi: pressed and flat-shaped sushi

Saba: mackerel

Saké: rice wine

Sake: salmon

San-mai oroshi: three-fillet cut for a fish

Sashimi: raw fish, served without rice

Shamoji: rice paddle

Shiso: Japanese basil

Shoyu: soy sauce

Su: rice vinegar

Sushi-meshi: sushi rice

Sushi-zu: spiced, sweetened vinegar

Tai: sea bream

Tako: octopus

Takuan: pickled daikon radish

Tamago: egg, or omlet in sushi terms

Temaki: hand-rolled sushi

Tempura: battered and deep fried dish

Teriyaki: grilled, broiled, or roasted ingredients cooked with a
sauce of soy sauce, mirin, and sugar

Umeboshi: sour plum pickles

Unagi: freshwater eel

Wakame: a kind of seaweed

Wasabi: Japanese horseradish